W9-BUJ-827

GET A GRIP!

BY
JOHN M. CAPOZZI

ILLUSTRATIONS BY
KIMBERLY SMITH
and
DAVID HARBAUGH

JMC Publishing Services
125 Brett Lane
Fairfield, CT 06430
2000

Copyright © 2001 by JMC Publishing Services

All rights reserved under International
and Pan-American Copyright Conventions.

Published in the United States by
JMC Publishing Services
A Division of JMC Industries, Inc.
125 Brett Lane
Fairfield, Connecticut 06430

All rights reserved. Written permission
must be secured from the publisher
to use or reproduce any part of this
book for any reason.

Library of Congress Cataloging-in-Publication
Data

Capozzi, John M.
GET A GRIP!

First Edition

p.   cm.
ISBN 0-9656410-5-8
1. Sports & Recreation   2.Humor
3. Crafts & Hobbies

98765432
First Edition

Printed in Canada.

This book is dedicated to my son, Peter, and my daughter, Meghan, whom I love so much. It is also dedicated to my amazing and beautiful wife who is totally responsible for my success in life and in business, who manages our financial affairs with great wisdom, and who also writes all of my dedications.

Other titles by John M. Capozzi

**Why Climb the Corporate Ladder
When You Can Take the Elevator? ***
500 Secrets for Success in Business and Life

**If You Want the Rainbow ...
You Gotta Put Up with the Rain! ***
500 Secrets for Success in Business and Life

A Spirit of Greatness;
Stories from the Employees of American Airlines

** 100% of the royalties from these books and
GET A GRIP! will be donated to educational
scholarship programs for children at-risk.*

To obtain one of John Capozzi's books:
visit your local bookstore
visit www.jmcpublishingservices.com
call: (800) 910-4944
from outside the U.S. and Canada (212) 439-4338
fax: (203) 255-4103
or mail your order to:
JMC Publishing Services
PO Box 1200
Southport, CT 06490

FOREWORD

I began writing ***GET A GRIP!*** for two reasons. My primary motivation was to create another vehicle to help raise additional funding for our educational scholarship programs for children at-risk. We must recognize that the future for both our families and our business community is directly and proportionately related to the quality of education that we provide our children. As I have with my other two best-selling business books, *Why Climb the Corporate Ladder When You Can Take the Elevator?* and *If You Want the Rainbow You Gotta Put Up with the Rain!* 100% of the royalties from the sale of the hardcover edition of ***GET A GRIP!*** will be donated to educational scholarship programs for children. The 21st Century brings with it new challenges. Business is becoming increasingly technology-reliant and much less restricted by geographical boundaries. Workers must be more literate in math, computer science, and general business skills to even survive in entry-level positions in today's aggressive and profit-conscious business community. As such, it is more critical than ever that we all maintain a personal commitment to the quality of education that we provide our children.

The second reason for my writing this book has been captured in our jacket quote by Neil DeFeo, CEO at Remington Products: "Golf is a wonderful game and this book helps to remind us not to take a great pleasure too seriously." For years I have noticed that many of my friends (and their spouses) take the game of golf extremely seriously. I'd even call some of them "excessive." I initially thought that writing a "fun" book about golf that can make you laugh at yourself, reduce "golf stress," and improve personal relations with your spouse, would put it all back into perspective. However, that changed when I was introduced to golf and found myself taking on these "excessive" qualities. The first time I successfully completed a "perfect" swing and my club solidly connected with the ball – I was hooked.

My friend, Peter Smith of International Management Group, had suggested that I take lessons at the new PGA Learning Center in Port St. Lucie, Florida. I agreed hesitantly and enlisted my son, Peter, to join me. We arrived for our first lesson at the Learning Center run by Rick Martino, a master professional at the PGA, along with two extraordinary instructors, Kevin Compare and Eric Johnson. Most of the eight golfers in our class had been playing for 15-20 years and simply wanted to take serious strokes off their game. My son and I were the only rank beginners. We worked for 3 days learning an amazing amount about the game of golf.

Following our intensive 3-day PGA training course we left the PGA Learning Center and drove to the Ocean Reef Club in Key Largo, Florida where we played nine holes with their head pro, Jim DeMallie. This is an incredible club and Jim is an incredible instructor. The next day we played the back nine at Ocean Reef again and I had one birdie, two pars, four bogeys and two "we will not talk about" holes! I couldn't believe my success. This is all to say that, with proper training, even a rank beginner can become a serious golfer in a very short period of time. Like many of my "excessive" friends, I am now hooked on golf!

I wish to thank more than a dozen of my "excessive" golf friends for their help in contributing so many of the items in *GET A GRIP!* I also wish to apologize to anyone who, inadvertently, was not properly credited. Some of the items in this book have been floating around clubhouses for years and I'm afraid that, in the re-telling, some of the originators of these bits of wisdom and humor may have been lost.

I hope you enjoy *GET A GRIP!* and I hope that this book relaxes you and your game a bit and allows you and your spouse to enjoy the game of golf even more … and isn't that really what it's all about?

ABOUT THE AUTHOR

John M. Capozzi is an accomplished entrepreneur, author and the President of JMC Industries, Inc.; JMC Investments, LLC; and JMC Publishing Services. During his corporate career with American Airlines and Midland Bank he was promoted 13 times in 13 years. He left corporate America as an Executive Vice President to start his own investment firm in 1979.

In addition to his entrepreneurial efforts, Mr. Capozzi was a member of the Organizing Committee for the *Presidents' Summit for America's Future*, now called *America's Promise*, chaired by General Colin Powell; serves on the board of *Operation Independence*, now known as *BNI*, a joint venture between the Government of Israel and the U.S. Government dedicated to helping Israel to become economically independent; and is also a board member of the *National Peace Garden* for which former presidents George Bush and Jimmy Carter serve as honorary co-chairmen. Mr. Capozzi is also currently generating funding for the *Points of Light Foundation* started by former President Bush.

Mr. Capozzi is the author of two best-selling business maxim books, *Why Climb the Corporate Ladder When You Can Take the Elevator?* and *If You Want the Rainbow You Gotta Put Up with the Rain!* written to help businesspeople focus on what it takes to become successful in business and in life. 100% of the royalties from these two books and ***GET A GRIP!*** are donated to educational scholarship programs for children at-risk. A new maxim taken from these collections appears each day on his web site www.maximoftheday.com.

Mr. Capozzi is also the author of *A Spirit of Greatness; Stories from the Employees of American Airlines*. *Spirit* is a blueprint for any corporation interested in motivating their employees to provide better service to their customers.

Mr. Capozzi is credited with the creation of the highly successful Mini-Book[SM] premium concept, allowing sponsors to give away mini versions of his business books, and books on a variety of other topics, to highly targeted recipients. The books offer an extremely low CPM and high pass-along/retention rate. More than 100 major corporations are currently utilizing advertising space in Mr. Capozzi's Mini-Books[SM].

Mr. Capozzi currently serves as a director on the board of various organizations, corporations and schools. In addition to his business activities he has been a keynote speaker for various business organizations and has authored several columns about business success for business publications. Mr. Capozzi has appeared on both the *Today* show and *Good Morning America*. He resides in Connecticut with his wife and two children.

GET A GRIP!

BY
JOHN M. CAPOZZI

ILLUSTRATIONS BY
KIMBERLY SMITH
and
DAVID HARBAUGH

"You miss 100% of the shots
you never take."
— *Wayne Gretzky*

Achieving a certain level
of success in golf is only
important if you can finally
enjoy the level you've
reached after you've
achieved it.

"I'd rather be lucky
than good."
— *Branch Rickey*

Golf is one of those very
rare sports that gives you
ample time and opportunity
to defeat yourself.

Do you tense up on the tough holes? Try washing your ball on the tee with the huge water hazard.

3

Some people will try almost anything
to save a stroke.

"The best wood in most amateurs' bags is the pencil."
— *Chi Chi Rodriguez*

In golf, marginal tactics executed passionately will almost always outperform brilliant tactics executed marginally.

"Golf is a game of
effortless power, not
powerless effort."
— *Bob Toski*

If your best shots are the
practice swing and the
"gimme putt," you might wish
to reconsider this game.

"Golf has to be dealt with
on two levels. The
mechanics are useless if the
emotions run amok."
— *Frank Hannigan*

If you find you do not mind playing golf
in the rain, the snow, even during a
hurricane, here's a valuable tip: your life
is in trouble.

Golf is the only sport
where the most feared
opponent is yourself.

Take comfort knowing that
in golf as in life, things
almost always turn out other
than one anticipates.

"If I needed advice from my caddie, he'd be hitting the shots and I'd be carrying the bag."
— *Bobby Jones*

You never have to play your
best game to win … you just
have to shoot the lowest score.

"Ed, thanks for loaning Ernie that
Cure Your Slice video ..."

To really learn about a person's character, play golf with them.

"If you watch a game, it's fun.
If you play it, it's recreation.
If you work at it, it's golf."
— *Bob Hope*

People who lose their
tempers are the ones who
usually lose their matches.

A low handicap is related
to concentration on the present,
not the future, not the past.

"Golf is the most over-taught and least-learned human endeavor. If they taught sex the way they teach golf, the human race would have died out years ago."
— *Jim Murray*

Sometimes it's better
to just play another ball.

Did you ever notice how badly you played the hole right after you asked the folks ahead if you could play through?

"Most people's golf is continually clouded by fear. They are afraid of errors – errors that inevitably occur."
– *Vivien Saunders*

When visiting a major tournament
don't follow the leaders.
They play a game you'll never play.
Instead, follow the tour rookies.
They get in more trouble
which you may find familiar.

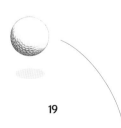

"Your golf buddy shot a 68
Saturday. He just faxed his
scorecard … it says,
'Suitable for framing.'"

"A round of golf is a struggle against a terrifying horde of weaknesses."
— *Leslie Schor*

If you keep doing what you're doing, you'll keep getting what you're getting.

"Golf's a hard game to figure.
One day you'll go out and slice it
and shank it, hit into all the traps
and miss every green.
The next day you go out and for
no reason at all you really stink."
— *Bob Hope*

In football it's the knees,
in hockey it's the teeth, in
golf it's the ulcers.

"The trick is never to give
up playing like a kid. The
more you play the more
complicated you try to make
it. You've got to keep
thinking young."
— *Gene Littler*

It's a bad day when your
slice hits another golfer …
it's a really bad day when
you discover he's a lawyer.

Your game will improve only
when you believe it can.

"Golf! You hit down to
make the ball go up. You
swing left and the ball goes
right. The lowest score
wins. And on top of that,
the winner buys the drinks."
— *Toots Shor*

The goal of every golfer
should be to live long
enough to shoot his or her age.

"The reason it's called
golf is that all the other
four letter words were
already taken."
— *Dr. Vincent Manjoney*

"If a lot of people gripped
a knife and fork the way
they do a golf club, they
would starve to death."
— *Sam Snead*

If your divot consistently
travels farther than your ball,
consider reading as a pastime.

In most sports the winner
is determined by who scores
the most points. In golf,
the winner is the one who
makes the fewest mistakes.

"It's hard to beat a person
who never gives up."
— *Babe Ruth*

In life as in golf … hit
the shot you know you can
hit. Not the one you think
you should hit.

Play happy and you'll
play better.

"Never bet with anyone you
meet on the first tee who
has a deep suntan and a
1-iron in his bag."
— *Dave Marr*

"I don't know how anybody can get that
worked up watching a golf match ..."

"You've just got one problem.
You stand close to the ball ...
after you've hit it."
— *Sam Snead*

"Golf is the most fun you
can have without taking off
your clothes."
— *Chi Chi Rodriguez*

Unless you're trying to
make a diamond from a hunk
of coal — lose the
pressure. It won't help
your golf game.

"I play in the low 80s.
If it's any hotter than that,
I won't play."
— *Joe E. Lewis*

Golf is quite difficult for
seriously overweight
people. If you tee your
ball where you can hit it,
you can't see it. If you
tee your ball where you can
see it, you can't hit it.

"Tee your ball high ...
air offers less resistance than dirt."
– *Jack Nicklaus*

"Nothing wrong with golf
that a good depression
wouldn't cure."
— *Dan Jenkins*

If you focus very hard on
how bad your last shot was,
guess what, your next shot
will be worse.

"Golf is not a game of how far.
It's a game of how near."
— *Bob Toski*

"I don't take my swing out
of town. If it breaks down,
I may not be able to get parts."
– *Kaye Kessler*

If you have re-gripped your
golf ball retriever more
than once you might question
if this game is really for you.

Why is it that when you tell yourself,
"Don't hit it in the water"
your body only seems to hear
the word "water"?

If you can't break 100,
don't play golf with your boss.

Golf is like a bank ... you
can't take out what you
haven't put in.

"A perfect shot fills the eye
and is a thing of beauty."
— *Jerome Travis*

A tragedy of the game is
that you can never look up
to watch a great shot.

If a foursome requests to
"play through" your twosome
... you should just go home.

"I ran over his driver in the garage by
mistake. It actually corrected his slice ..."

"Putts get real difficult
the day they pass the money out."
— *Lee Trevino*

"Golf is like a love affair.
If you don't take it seriously, it's not fun.
If you take it too seriously,
it breaks your heart."
— *Anonymous*

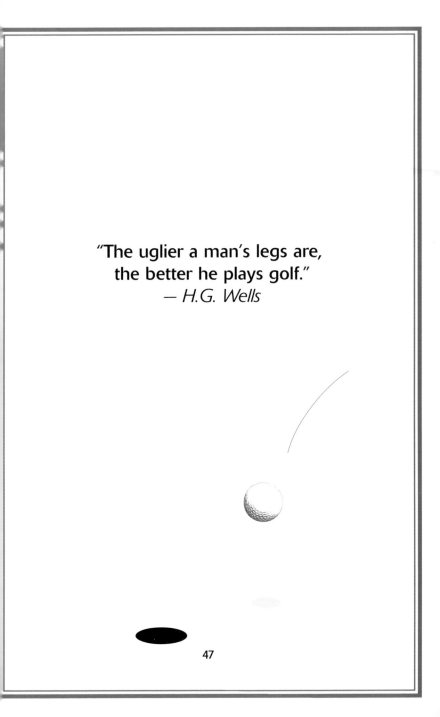

"The uglier a man's legs are,
the better he plays golf."
— *H.G. Wells*

"I hope you're not going to do this
every time you make a
hole-in-one!"

You should establish a
personal rule that you will
just go home after 4 hours
on the course … no matter
what hole you're on.

"It's good sportsmanship to
not pick up lost golf balls
while they are still rolling."
— *Mark Twain*

The most difficult part of
the golf game is learning
not to talk about it.

Remember ... putters don't float.

If you find that you are
spending more on golf
lessons than you do on your
children's education, you
should seek professional help.

"A good swing begins with a
good grip."
– *Tom Watson*

"Golf is a non-violent game
played violently from within."
— *Bob Toski*

To play better golf, don't
add up your score until
you've finished the round.

"I'll be at a seminar on stress ..."

"Golf is harder than baseball. In golf, you have to play your foul balls."
— *Ted Williams*

Losers quit when they are tired, winners quit when they have won.

If you have ever mentioned your golf game in prayers at church, you might also wish to consider psychiatric help.

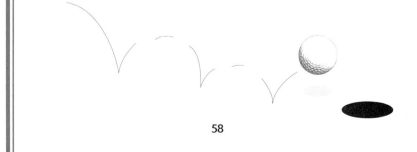

"In golf, great hitters don't always have an advantage: remember a two-foot putt counts the same as a 300-yard drive."
— *Jack Nicklaus*

59

If you have lost more than four balls
on any given hole, for safety reasons,
let your partner drive the cart.

The members who command the
best service at your golf
club either have the lowest
handicaps or the highest bar bills.

"If a man is notified that he has been appointed to serve on the rules committee for his club tournament, he should instantly remember that he must attend an important business meeting in Khartoum."
— *Herbert Warren Wind*

If you beat your boss at golf, he probably will want to play again … if he doesn't, you're probably fired and it doesn't matter.

"There is nothing sadder in this life than the spectacle of husband and wife with practically equal handicaps drifting apart."
— *P.G. Wodehouse*

"Just before hitting the ball, I think about where I want it to go."
— *Tiger Woods*

You know your golf game is improving when you start missing shots much closer than you used to.

The term "mulligan" is
really a contraction of the
phrase "maul it again."

"Thinking must be the
hardest thing we do in golf,
because we do so little of it."
— *Harvey Penick*

"... when your husband left for the golf course wearing orange and green knickers, a purple shirt, yellow sweater, blue shoes, and a magenta cap, did you notice anything unusual?"

"Pressure is playing for
ten dollars when you've only
got five in your pocket."
– *Lee Trevino*

You can always tell luck
from skill by the duration
of your success.

"Hit the ball with a
purpose instead of a foggy hope."
— *Tommy Armour*

Golf is a game of choices.
You can choose to look up
and hit a really ugly shot
or you can choose to keep
your head down and not see
where your ball went.

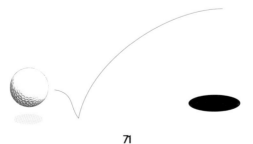

"We're not sure what new
technology we will be using
in the clubs next year ... we
just know the price will be
$1,200 each."

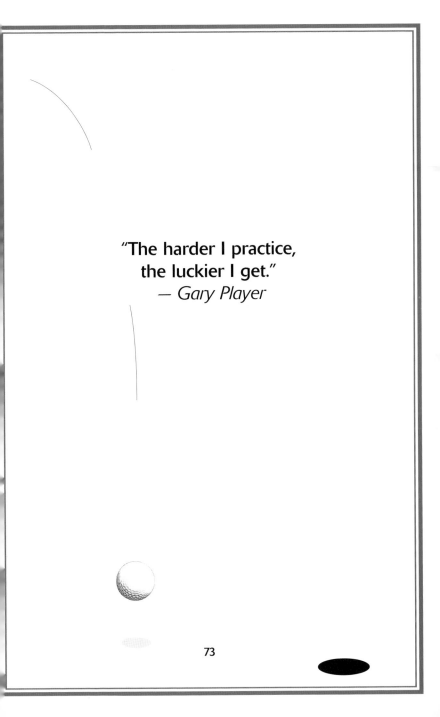

"The harder I practice,
the luckier I get."
— *Gary Player*

73

The longer you take to hit
a putt the more you can
think of ways to miss it.

An interesting thing about
golf is that no matter how
badly you play, it is always
possible to get worse.

"Playing with your spouse on the golf course is about as great a risk to your marriage as playing with someone else's spouse anywhere else."
— *Peter Andre*

My doctor told me that learning to play golf
would relax me and add ten years to my life.
He was absolutely right … I took up golf
and I immediately feel ten years older.

Why is it twice as
difficult to hit a ball over
water than sand?

"Golf is an awkward set of
bodily contortions designed
to produce a graceful result."
— *Tommy Armour*

"It's not whether you win
or lose … it's whether I win
or lose."
— *Anonymous*

Many Wall Street brokers
believe that a stroke does not really
occur unless it is observed by
more than one person.

The die-hard golfer rolled over
and nudged his sleeping wife
early Sunday morning ...

"What'll it be?
Golf course or intercourse?"

With a sparkle in her eye
she leaned in,

" ... don't forget your sweater."

"I'm not saying my golf game
is bad but if I grew tomatoes,
they'd come up sliced."
— *Miller Barber*

"I wish I could play my
normal game … just once."
— *Anonymous*

They say you must relax and
empty your mind to play
great golf. Does this mean
mindless people play better golf?

"The score a player reports
on any hole should always be
regarded as his opening offer."
— *Henry Beard*

If the "foot wedge" is your most valuable
club ... perhaps you don't really
understand the game.

"You can't think and hit
at the same time."
— *Yogi Berra*

If exercise is so good for
us, why do so many
professional athletes retire
at age thirty-five?

A "gimme" can best be
defined as an agreement
between two golfers ...
neither of whom can putt
very well.

Even a bad day on the
course is better than a good
day at the office.

Most accidents occur in the
home. Golfers know this and
that's why they seek the
safety of the golf course on
the weekends.

It is correct etiquette to advise
anyone on the golf course with a cell phone
that they are a complete jerk.

"Type A" golfers are people who let pressing foursomes play through … and then speed up their game.

"Give me good clubs, fresh air
and a beautiful partner ...
and you can keep my clubs
and the fresh air."
— *Jack Benny*

Golf is like a marriage: If you take yourself too seriously it won't work ... and both are expensive.

Golf is one of only two things in life you can enjoy without being good at … the other is sex.

"Golf's three ugliest words:
still your shot."
— *Dave Marr*

To some golfers, the
greatest handicap is the
ability to add correctly.

"You never own golf; it's only on loan, so enjoy it while you can."
— *Kenneth Blanchard*

Only a stupid golfer throws
his club behind him. The
smart golfer throws his club
ahead so he can pick it up
on the way to the next hole.

"Swing easy. Hit hard."
— *Julius Boros*

A scorecard is often
identified as a "printed
form on which golfers record
their lies."

If it bothers you that you
lose lots of golf balls,
consider bowling ... the ball
always comes back.

Follow the rule:
If your shot is "between clubs"
always choose the longer club.
You won't feel the need to swing
so hard and only a perfect shot
with the shorter club will get you home.

"Someone stole your driver? That solves one of your problems!"

"Reach for the stars and
you'll rarely come up with
mud in your hand."
– *Leo Burnett*

"If you think it's hard to
meet new people, try picking
up the wrong golf ball."
— *Jack Lemmon*

No matter how much money you spend on high-tech equipment, remember, a bad swing will result in a bad shot.

"If profanity had an
influence on the flight of
the ball, the game would be
played far better than it is."
– *Horace Hutchinson*

"He just took a full golf
swing in his cubicle ..."

Playing golf doesn't take
time away from your life ...
it puts life into your time.

People who work through a
little pain will always
experience a little progress.

"The next best thing to
playing and winning is
playing and losing.
The main thing is to play."
— *Nick "The Greek" Dandalos*

People who consistently lay
up short of front-facing bunkers
are the same ones who stop suddenly
when the traffic light first turns yellow.

Do you own a variety of golf hats?
If so, are any brightly colored?
Do any have bobbles on the top?
If you own a fur golf hat please
stop reading this book immediately,
walk to the nearest window and jump.

"The real reason your pro
tells you to keep your head
down is so you can't see him
laughing at you."
— *Phyllis Diller*

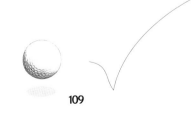

"Always learn from the skillful.
He who teaches himself
hath a fool for his master."
— *Ben Franklin*

The Golfer's Prayer

God, grant me patience ... right now.

In golf, training tells you
exactly what to do ...
confidence allows you to do it.

"I'd really like to hear more ...
but he's obviously guilty."

"My game is improving…
I am hitting fewer spectators."
— *Former President Gerald Ford*

"The smart golfer always
tries to hit his second shot
the first time."
— *Hugh Ganley*

In golf, some people tend
to get confused with all the
numbers … they shoot a
"six," yell "fore" and write "five."

"Hey, Hon, I left early.
Let's play nine …"

"There are some shots that
cannot be endured with a
club still in your hand."
— *Bobby Jones*

"Golf is a better game
played downhill."
– *Jack Nicklaus*

Mark your golf balls. It's
really annoying to hit the
wrong ball ... it's right up
there with driving off in
someone else's cart.

If you remember only the good shots after a round, you are an idealist. If you remember only the bad ones you're a masochist. If you remember both, you're a manic-depressive.

"What kind of fool would be
running in this weather?"

"The real fun of golf is in
the improving."
— *Ben Hogan*

Falling in love with golf
can be far more expensive
than a marriage, far more
serious than a job, and far
more humbling than anything.

To obtain a marriage
license, couples should be
required to play golf with
each other at least once.

Try not to play with people
whose golf repertoire
includes terms such as
"whack it" or "forget about it."

Some golfers believe "overclubbing"
can be corrected by "overlooking"
or "undercounting." When using a caddie
it can also be corrected by "overtipping."

If you find yourself pleased that you
locate more balls in the rough than you
actually have lost, your focus is totally
wrong and your personality might not be
right for golf ... it is also just a matter of
time before the IRS investigates your business.

"He who has the fastest golf cart
never has a bad lie."
— *Mickey Mantle*

Golf can best be defined as
an endless series of
tragedies obscured by the
occasional miracle.

"Bets lengthen putts and
shorten drives."
— *Henry Beard*

It does not matter how
slowly your game improves,
only that it continues to
improve.

"I'd give up golf
if I didn't have so many
sweaters."
— *Bob Hope*

"... I don't see any ball ... I gotta get
back to work."

"The worst hole at Pebble
Beach is like being the
ugliest Miss America."
— *Rick Reilly*

Take care of your golf equipment.
Remember, you don't have to
brush all of your teeth either ...
only the ones you want to keep.

"If you drink, don't drive ...
don't even putt."
— *Dean Martin*

If the grass around your home is longer
than the rough at your course, your
marriage may be in trouble.

Analyze the situation before
making critical golf shots.
General George Armstrong Custer received
information that a number of Indians
were gathering at Little Big Horn.
Without analyzing the situation he
decided to ride out with 250 men
to "surround" the almost 3,000 Indians …
this was a major bogey.

"Every shot makes somebody happy."
— *Gary Player*

Tailors are known for saying,
"measure twice ... cut once."
It works the same in golf.

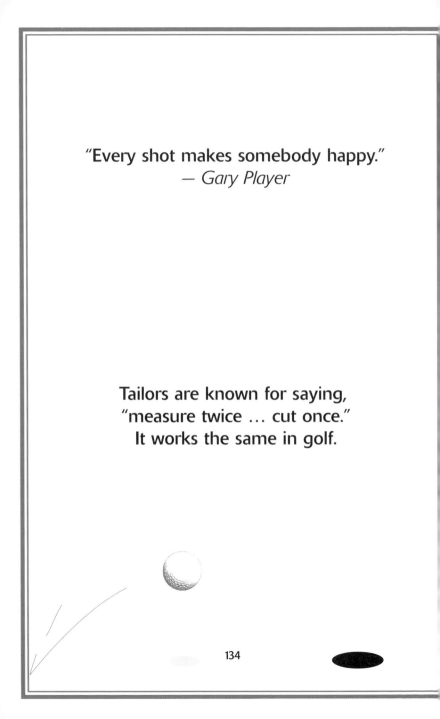

Sometimes when a golfer with
money meets a golfer with experience,
the golfer with experience ends up with
the money and the golfer with
the money ends up with experience.

Why doesn't a stick or pebble
in the path of a putt ever
cause the ball to go in?

"Practice does not make
perfect … only perfect
practice makes perfect."
— *Vince Lombardi*

In golf, as in life, if you
think you can, you can, and
if you think you can't,
you're right.

"You need a purpose in mind
when you practice."
— *David Leadbetter*

Golfers who try to make
everything perfect before
taking the shot rarely make
a perfect shot.

Four golfers playing together is a "foursome," two is a "twosome," why isn't one a "lonesome"?

"No sales yet, boss ... but I'm doin' a lot
of pitchin'."

"No one becomes a champion
without help."
— *Johnny Miller*

In golf, amateurs practice
until they can get it right …
professionals practice until
they can't get it wrong.

141

Success in golf isn't related to the number of good strokes taken … it's related to the number of bad strokes not taken.

"Prayer never seems to work
for me on the golf course.
I think this has something
to do with my being a
terrible putter."
— *Rev. Billy Graham*

"Yes, I do have an accent ... but one of the most embarrassing moments was when I asked my caddie for a sand wedge and ten minutes later he came back with a ham on rye."
– *Chi Chi Rodriguez*

"Ninety-five percent of the putts
you leave short don't go in."
— *Hubert Green*

The next time you hit a bad
shot consider the hockey
player … he hits a bad shot
and 15,000 fans "boo" him.

"I don't care to join any
club that's prepared to have
me as a member."
– *Groucho Marx*

Golf is a game of learning.
When you stop learning,
you should stop playing.

"In my opinion, the average
golfer underestimates himself."
— *Ben Hogan*

Middle age is most disturbing.
You are too young to have
the time to play golf and
too old to rush the net.

147

"Golf combines two favorite American pastimes: taking long walks and hitting things with a stick."
— *P.J. O'Rourke*

One under par is called a
"birdie,"
Two under par is called an
"eagle,"
Three under par is called
"bull."

"The woods are full of long drivers."
— *Harvey Penick*